MOVING INTO THE NEW ME

....BY FAITH

RAYNA STEPHENS
Formerly Rayna Roxanne

CJ3 Publishing LLC, Snellville, GA

©2019 Rayna Stephens. All rights Reserved.

No part of this book may be reproduced, stored in a retrieval system, or transmitted by any means without the prior written permission of the author.

First published by CJ3 Publishing LLC   10/15/2019

CJ3 Publishing LLC

2330 Scenic Highway, Ste 503

Snellville, GA 30039

ISBN: 978-0-578-52378-1(sc)

ISBN 978-0-578-56910-9(Ebook)

Library of Congress Control Number: 2019906606

Book cover design by JOY (Fiverr: pro_designer123)

Printed in the United States of America

All imagery in this book is original © Rayna Stephens

Because of the dynamic nature of the internet, any web addresses or links contained in this book may have changed since publication and may no longer be valid. The views expressed in this work are solely those of the author and do not necessarily reflect the views of the publisher, and the publisher hereby disclaims any responsibility for them.

FOREWORD

In a world of incredible challenges and full of acceptable substitutions, "Moving Into the New Me....By Faith" establishes the importance of a strong spiritual base, one dedicated to prayer.

Rayna Stephens, through her own personal journey of struggle and strength, has masterfully given valuable keys and insight on how to overcome when all seems hopeless.

This book gives the reader a reason to hope again; to believe that through persistence and faith in their God given call, life might cause them to bend but their purpose won't allow them break.

Pastor Eugene "G" Whitmore

Network of Believers Int., Little Rock, AR

Life Coach

ACKNOWLEDGMENTS

First and foremost, I have to give my Heavenly Father all of the glory and honor for what He has done for me! I am extremely grateful that He has given me this opportunity to minister to His people, thru my writing.

I must thank my friend, Kevin, who has stood thru some challenging storms with me. The help you gave to me and my family is greatly appreciated and will never be forgotten. God bless you.

Next, I want to thank Pastor Eugene "G" Whitmore and First Lady, "Lady T", who blesses my soul thru "Lunch Time Uplift" ministry that broadcast on Face Book Live every Monday, Wednesday and Friday. Their ministry continues to give me strength to go thru the seasons of my journey.

Also, I must acknowledge my beautiful and tenacious cousin, LaRhonda Hardy. She inspired me to keep walking thru my challenges while, at the same time, walking thru her own. And, I want to thank my mother for helping me, in a season, when others had given up on me. I am truly grateful, to you, for all that you do. I love both of you dearly.

And finally, to the best gifts of my life; to my awesome children, words cannot even explain how much I love you. You all have always been by my side and have weathered the storms with me. The love you genuinely have, for me, is indisputably remarkable! Thank you for always loving and supporting me, despite it all! And to my four grandsons, you are my JOY....period!

With Love,

Ray

Table of Contents

Foreword iii
Acknowledgments iv
Chapter 1: Accepting The Call 1
Chapter 2: Awakening 3
The God of Creation 7
Chapter 3: But God....Amazing Grace 9
Amazed 11
Chapter 4: Faith Pleases God 13
Extraordinary Assignment 19
Chapter 5: It Is Necessary 21
Watch This! 25
Chapter 6: The *Eviction* Process 27
When I Surrendered 31
Chapter 7: The Writ Executed 35
Set Free 39
Chapter 8: Protection Thru The Process 41
I've Been Kept 45
Chapter 9: It Only Looks Broken 47
Nature 53
Chapter 10: The *Limbo* Period 55
The God of Your Word 59
Chapter 11: Comfort In The Crying Times 61
My Soul Provider 65
Chapter 12: Standing On His Promises 67
Reflections 71

Chapter 13: Winner 73
Thru It All Trust God 77
Chapter 14: Moving Into The New Me 79
Sound Direction 83
Chapter 15: ....By Faith 87
Crazy Faith 91
Special Dedication 95
Book Review 97
Bibliography 101
Order Information 103

~~~~~~

Trusting in the Most High God and the works He has done and continues to do for you, thru His son, is an effort that should be an everyday priority in your life's journey.

~~~~~~

Chapter 1

Accepting The Call

My Version of Faith:

Complete Trust (to know without a doubt) and obedience in the Heavenly Father that ALL things desired by Him, according to His will and purpose for our lives, WILL manifest and come to pass!

FAITH…This is a subject that is extremely dear and sensitive to my heart. It has taken me quite some time to finally begin to write about it. When my Heavenly Father instructed me to evangelize, I ran from the calling for several years. It was when I lost my oldest children's father in a fatal motorcycle accident that I finally surrendered, completely, unto the Lord. I will never forget that day.

It was August 29, 2013, and I was sitting on the side of my bed still in disbelief, after a few weeks had passed, that he was gone. In that moment is when I heard a still small whisper in my ear that said, "It could have been you." Right then I said to the Lord, "Yes, I accept your call, Father; whatever you want me to do, I'll do it." I did not know, at the time, what He had specifically chosen for me to do. All I knew was my life had become His vessel. It was not until October of the same year when someone had doubted a decision I had made for my family, that my ministry had become clear to me………FAITH.   Romans 8:30-31

~~~~~~~~~~~~~~~~~~~~~~~~~~~~~~~~~~~~

Father, we know we could never be who You are; yet, please allow who you are to dwell within us, forever!

~~~~~~~~~~~~~~~~~~~~~~~~~~~~~~~~~~~~

Chapter 2

Awakening

When you tap into the Father's Power that is within you, you will discover who you really are. You will also discover your true strength and character. You will be reminded of where you come from and whose you are, and the power that is within you to subdue and call things that are not, into manifestation. Divine wisdom and knowledge will be unleashed and revealed in and thru you. Your creativeness and divine abilities that have been dormant will come alive and be restored to you. The Father's Holy Truth will shine, with radiance, thru your vessel! Nothing will be able to stop the manifestation of the Heavenly Father's power that works thru you! It will cause the spirit of those who does not have a relationship with the Lord to, either, draw into you....into the Holy Spirit that is within you, or to flee from you!

Wake up people! God's Word says we are more than conquerors. It also says we are the head and not the tail....we are above and not beneath. So why are you continuously being gullible and accepting all the worldly deceptions that are introduced to you? Can't you see that it is a setup, by the enemy, to continue to distract you from who you really are and the power you possess within? The world cannot afford for you to discover your worth because, if you do, it would lose control, and God's righteousness would prevail thru-out the entire land, which is definitely going to happen, regardless. So why not become a part of the kingdom movement?

You cry out to the Heavenly Father, asking Him to help you, when He has given you the power to *speak* VICTORY over your life and over your circumstances. Why? Because He is in you! YOU ARE VICTORY because the VICTOR dwells within you! Tap into His power and not the "so called" power that the world is

deceiving you with; such as the love of materialism, superficial thoughts and ways, idol gods, homosexuality, fear, etc. The Lord's power is where you will find your deliverance and your freedom. It is not far at all. Just dig a little deeper, within yourself, and there it will be revealed and restored to you, in Jesus name, Amen.
1Corithians 15:57; Deuteronomy 28:13; Romans 8:37

~~~~~~~~~~~~~~~~~~~~~~~~~~~~~~~~~~~

You were not created with words.
You were created in His image
and by His Spirit...Walk in it...
...By Faith!

~~~~~~~~~~~~~~~~~~~~~~~~~~~~~~~~~~~

~~~~~~~~~~~~~~~~~~~~~~~~~~~~

*Everyday will not be a great day for us
BUT GOD will always be great EVERYDAY!*

~~~~~~~~~~~~~~~~~~~~~~~~~~~~

The God of Creation

You are the creator of the Earth
which is a temporary dwelling place
You are the creator of man
whom you put here to fill its space

You are the creator of dominion
which, to man, you gave power
You are the creator of protection which
cares for us every minute and hour

You are the creator of peace
that is manifested within our souls
You are the creator of the heart
which joy so freely overflows

You are the creator of the
mind which is used to discern
You are the creator of wisdom which
teaches divine knowledge in return

You are the creator of the eye
which is the lamp of the body
You are the creator of the spirit
in which our vessel embodies

You are the creator of the
limbs which produces activity
You are the creator of
giving also known as charity

You are the creator of music
and the bells that ring
You are the creator of all
beings and the songs they sing

You are the creator of the rain
which falls so pure and divine
You are the creator of the sun
which empowers the day to shine

You are the creator of the
wind and the air we breathe
You are the creator of the
flowers, the trees and the leaves

You are the creator of all plans
which leads into our destiny
You are the creator of Heaven
where we will live thru-out eternity

April 22, 2011
Genesis 1:1

Chapter 3

But God....Amazing Grace

God's grace keeps us each and every day. When we woke up, this morning, it was not because we have done it on our own. It was not because we have been so perfect in the flesh that we deserve to be alive. It is only by the Heavenly Father's amazing grace.

The grace of God provides blessings we have not, by far, even earned. He gives to us, generously, because He loves us so much. Grace is His unmerited favor poured out into our lives. Grace carries us thru the extremely challenging journeys when we do not have the strength to carry ourselves. Grace is the substance of God's love for His children. His grace forgives us; and it gives us strength to forgive ourselves and others, as well. Grace gives us chance after chance to get it right. Think about it…..when we walk outside the will of God, and we know that what we have done is wrong, we began to feel bad. We feel like there is no way we can fix what we have made a mess of. But God!! His grace says, "I love you and I forgive you." Not only does He forgive our shortcomings, He also gracefully allows similar opportunities so we may repent, reconcile and redeem ourselves with Him. God loves us so much that He is willing to go above and beyond for us to abide in His righteousness.

God's grace sustains us thru the weakest moments in our lives. His grace empowers us with His strength, when we are at our lowest, to keep persevering. His grace grants us the ability to operate in His wisdom and discernment. His grace makes provisions for us and sustains us in our everyday needs. God's grace provides His spirit of protection to keep us in the most dangerous situations. His grace heals us of our afflictions and infirmities. His grace renews our mind and keeps it sound. By His grace, thru our Faith……it is even by His grace that we have the ability to operate in our Faith. Every situation we come thru is by God's Amazing Grace!

If you think for one moment that *you* are the reason why you are financially blessed, healthy, intelligent, etc, you should really take some time to yourself to reflect and reevaluate your thoughts. Think back on the times when you did not know how you were going to make it thru the week because you had no money to your name, but you made it thru.... God's grace! Think back on the times when you were in pain and the medication the doctor gave to you did not help; but one early morning you woke up feeling brand new.... God's grace! Think back on the times when you had issues with your child and you were about to throw in the towel because you did not know what else to do; but then one morning that child came to you, in tears, apologizing for what he or she had done.... God's grace! Think back on the times you were driving thru the stop sign or traffic light and a speeding car was headed straight for you but, somehow, they had just missed hitting your car by inches.... God's grace! Think back on the times that you had a shut off notice (now you know you have had one a time or two…. stop fronting!) and you had one day to pay it but you did not get paid for three more days; and someone you had not heard from, in years, called and said that God had put it in his spirit to send you money.... God's grace! You may not have experienced all of these instances, but I am sure I have covered at least one that you have encountered. If it had not been for our God's AMAZING GRACE……!

The Heavenly Father is our creator and He knew everything we were going to experience, in this lifetime, before we entered into this world. His grace allows us to be here, and it is His grace that will continue to keep us. By His grace, thru FAITH, we are able to become and accomplish everything He has ordained for our lives and His glory. God's grace is our sustainer! Take it from me, the person who is sitting here at a hotel table writing this book to you. God's grace is definitely our sustainer, in Jesus name. Amen. John 1:16-17

Amazed

I am amazed at the things
you faithfully do and say
Amazed how you keep
me safe from day to day

I am amazed at your strength
and your glorious power
Amazed how you keep
me thru my darkest hour

I am amazed at your precious
grace, compassion and mercy
Amazed how you bring me
thru my worldly controversy

I am amazed at your undeniable
glory because it shines so bright
Amazed how you take the
wrong in me and make it right

I am amazed at your provisions
and how you always supply
Amazed how you take the
smallest and make it multiply

I am amazed at your Holy
Spirit who lives deep within me
Amazed how you walk with me
on my most challenging journeys

I am amazed at your sweet
holiness and your sovereignty
Amazed how you bless my spirit
with richness when in poverty

I am amazed at your unmerited
favor for it has infinite length
Amazed how you keep me in
good health and your strength

I am amazed at your humbleness
when you died at man's hand
Amazed how you were buried
And with all power you rose again

I am amazed at your forgiveness
and salvation you give so freely
Amazed how you died on the
cross to save a lost wretch like me

October 14, 2011
Psalm 71:19

CHAPTER 4

FAITH PLEASES GOD

As you know, this book is about Faith and a testimony of life experiences that my family and I have endured. I am opening up my heart and pouring out some of my life's trials and challenges to minister and testify to those who are experiencing what I have been thru; and to minister to you about our Heavenly Father's unfailing love and His faithfulness He bestows upon us, when we put ALL of our TRUST in Him. I am writing this book of Faith in hopes of awakening the spirits of God's Kingdom children so those who do not have a relationship with Him may draw close, and for others even closer to the Father, to realize how deceived we have been, by this worldly system.

It can be very challenging to make a move of faith. There are a plethora of reasons why excuses are made not to take the first step of faith....the biggest reason is fear. At times, fear causes many delays to your blessings because you cannot fully comprehend the instruction, the process and the outcome even when the Lord has spoken victory over the situation. Fear IS NOT of neither the Heavenly Father's spirit nor His character. The enemy loves when you walk in fear; because when you do so, you cannot operate in the total capacity of your Faith. You may get nervous, at times, but the key is to ignite your faith in the One who said He would never leave or forsake us and allow it to conquer all fear, in Jesus name.

The Word says, "....If ye have faith as a grain of mustard seed, ye shall say unto this mountain, remove hence to yonder place; and it shall remove; and nothing shall be impossible unto you (Matthew 17:20 NIV)." As a young adult, I remember hearing this particular verse many times. And when I began to seriously become more intimate with my Heavenly Father, I constantly prayed and meditated about what this verse really meant. I used to wonder why Jesus used the parable *as a grain of mustard seed.* So, I was moved to research the mustard seed and found that it is the tiniest seed of the green plants and can grow to be—when it is nurtured—30 feet tall. As I continued to read the information about the seed, God gave me a revelation. I was shown that Jesus used the parable of the mustard seed because, although it is a very tiny seed, it does not stay that way. It grows to be the tallest green plant! I believe, in my spirit, Jesus was saying that our faith, in the Heavenly Father, should grow the very same way. He came and demonstrated a clear example of *complete dependency* upon his Father…our Father.

As you are nurtured in your intimate relationship with the Most High God, your faith in Him should be nurtured and grow, as well. And the more you come to know Him and experience His grace and favor, the more you should have confidence in His ability to bless above and beyond your expectations of Him. When you are learning about the greatness of God, the information is not just to be held in your mind, yet on the contrary, it is to be applied to your life's situations and challenges. Having confidence in the Lord is comparable to a college student who graduates with book knowledge in their specialized area of study. For instance, the graduate usually starts off as an entry level employee with no *hands-on* experience. I am sure that the new journey brings about nervousness and insecurities; but as time goes by and the more experience gained, the graduate becomes extremely confident in that particular field. Next thing you know (s)he is leading the meetings and training other entry level employees with absolute confidence in what (s)he has learned. It is the same thing with our Father! The more we learn about His sovereignty and character and the more we experience His favor, we should become more confident in His abilities. We should become more confident in HIM, period!

As God's children, we have got to get back to operating in the spirit of assurance and confidence.... Faith in God! I say *we* because I include myself, as well. I am not perfect, and at times, I must be reminded of my own ministry that God uses me for.... FAITH.

Faith, to me, is the belief in what we cannot see with our physical eye and what others say is the "impossible". There is absolutely nothing impossible for the Heavenly Father! I remember what my pastor (Pastor Eugene "G" Whitmore) said in one of his sermons.... He said, "You could NEVER make a request that exceeds God's ability to manifest!" Now that is powerful! It is just how infinite our Heavenly Father is! He is THE CREATOR of EVERYTHING! I remind myself of that truth, often, so I may be strengthened while I am on this journey. The Lord desires for us to trust Him to supply our needs just as our children trust us to supply their needs. He desires for all of us to live in royalty because He is Royalty. And if our God lives in us, then that is what He desires to overflow thru us....Royalty! We must know without a doubt He desires Royalty for us.

God is not a complicated God, no matter how much the adversary tries to portray the contrary. He is a loving, kind and compassionate God. He loves when we confide in Him and trust Him with our lives. He loves when we bring our problems and cares to Him and leave them there; because it becomes His opportunity to show us His supernatural abilities. He loves when we bring our broken hearts to Him and place them in His hands; because that becomes His opportunity to make them brand new! He loves when we consult with Him about our everyday challenges; because when we do, we are telling the Heavenly Father that we trust His profound wisdom and ability to make things right....to make them better, for His glory!

God desires the glory out of our lives, our situations and our circumstances. He desires the glory when He heals and when He makes a way out of what seems like no way at all. He desires to get the glory when He gives us supernatural blessings; and when we are in our challenges. Because when we glorify God thru the process, we express to Him that no matter what, we trust Him. He is extremely pleased with our total confidence in Him. He will move in such miraculous and marvelous ways when we execute our faith in Him, and Him alone!

Some years back, I had a next-door neighbor who I had built a very close relationship with. She would come over for dinner with me and my children. She had become a part of my family crew and there was nothing I would not do for her. So one day, we were talking and she began to tell me how her water bill was fifty dollars and how the water company was going to shut it off the next day because she did not have the money to pay it. While she was talking, all I could think about was how much I wanted to help her; but my water bill, which was the same amount, was due in three days and all I had was the money to pay for my bill. When she went back to her house, I began to genuinely pray for her, and then the unexpected happened! I heard the Holy Spirit say, "Give her the fifty dollars." Now, I know you can imagine how I was feeling at that moment. I opened my eyes so fast and was like, "God is that you talking to me, because you know my bill is due in three days, right?" I had become extremely nervous, so I jumped in my car and ran errands for a while. I was contemplating the instruction over and over; and finally, as I reversed my car into the driveway, I made peace with the situation and told the Lord, "YES, I will be obedient and trust You."

As soon as I turned my car off and put my hand on the door to exit, I received a phone call from my Uncle Albert whom I had not spoken to in, at least, three years. He said, "Hey there Morning Glory—that is my nick name he gave to me when I was a little girl—how are you?!" After I greeted him with such excitement, he said, "I've been collecting money from people who owed me, and the Holy Spirit spoke into my spirit and told me to send you fifty dollars!" My heart was so overwhelmed with amazement, gratefulness and joy that I could not even continue to talk to him! I said, "Unc, let me call you right back." I hung up my phone and shouted and praised God right there, in my car!

After I finished praising my Heavenly Father, I called my uncle back to express my gratefulness and appreciation to him. I told him what had happened, and he began to praise God with me! FAITH AND OBEDIENCE.... they go hand in hand! You see, God put my knowledge and faith, in Him, to the test. I would always minister to my neighbor about how the Lord will provide when we walk in obedience and faith in Him. His Word says, "Even so faith, if it hath not works, is dead, being alone." *Faith* is the trust we have in our Heavenly Father and the *Works* is the obedience to the instructions from our Father. If we cannot be obedient to the instructions He give to us, then our faith in Him is dead. If we trust God like we say we do, then we must trust in His mysterious ways and instructions, as well. Our blessings are poured out thru our obedience, by faith, to His divine instructions.

There is no way that I would have given my last fifty dollars for my bill some years prior to this instance! I was not mature enough, in my faith, to do so. It is a growth process—some take longer than others and some shorter; but the point is that we grow. The Lord does not want us to stay as a mustard seed. He desires for us to become the 30 feet plant! His grace, with your desire, will mature your faith. Never give up on God, because He NEVER gives up on you. Faith is the *key*; whether it is the mustard seed or the tall plant. God's grace excels us in His spirit; and He knows the exact moment we are ready to excel to the next realm of His glory. So, please do not look at the next person and feel that you should be abiding where they are. Stay focused on *your* relationship with the Heavenly Father and His grace, in your life, to mature your faith in Him. If you trust Him and Him alone, you will always come out on top, in Jesus name! Amen. Hebrews 11:6; Matthew 17:20; James 2:17

Be careful who you count out because of your judgment of their journey. Their destination is far greater than their walk!

EXTRAORDINARY ASSIGNMENT

God has graciously given an
extraordinary assignment to me
An assignment some will
look upon in disbelief

They will not believe in my assignment
because it is not in a worldly view
They will not believe in God's powers
and cannot give glory where it is due

God's spirit told me when I accept this
assignment, some people would not understand
And while on this assignment I will have
to put all my trust in Him and not in man

He told me on this assignment, the enemy will
try to attack and even try to make me doubt
But no matter the trial, stay focused on
Him, and He will direct me on this route

He told me that on this assignment I will
gain some friends and some friends I will lose
But this assignment will proceed the way
He ordered and not the way men choose

He showed me on this assignment, I will
experience disappointment and neglect
And it would be from those that I hold
close; the people I would never expect

He told me when I accept this assignment
I must go thru with His divine plans
And I must believe in the unseen
regardless of the circumstance

He told me He chose me so His
purpose for my life may be fulfilled
And for the years of suffering in His
name, His glory would be revealed

So God, I faithfully accept this extraordinary
assignment You so graciously gave to me
And I will fulfill Your assignment in faith and
obedience so others may see Your glory and believe

August 2, 2011
Exodus 14:15-16

CHAPTER 5

IT IS NECESSARY

It was about 6:12 am on June 15, 2017 when my Heavenly Father woke me up and I heard, "This is the time to make your request." I got up, went to the bathroom and went back to pray. My prayer request was different this time. I would usually pray and request for the "right now" deliverance, but not this time. This time I requested VICTORY! I requested victory over my mind, my body, my soul and my spirit. I requested victory over my finances and my circumstances…. VICTORY! I requested victory for all of God's children who had been trusting and faithful to Him. I stretched out across my bed and began to stare at the unique trees outside of my bedroom window, as I always would, in the early morning. I began to receive revelation about a distinct tree that I would often stare at, directly outside my office window, versus the other trees.

You see, the tree that was right outside my office window hardly ever shed its leaves during any season. Its leaves are very tough and durable; and they have withstood many harsh storms that barreled thru the area. A few days prior, I remember thinking while sitting at my desk, how I wanted my life to mimic that tree. At least I thought I did until the Lord showed me otherwise! Just when I thought I had it figured out is when the Lord showed me how much more His wisdom surpasses mine! I heard a quiet voice say, "What you are going thru, right now, is necessary." He told me that my children and other people were watching me. I heard, "Not having a job is necessary. This is an opportunity for me to show who I AM." And that is when He gave me the revelation of the trees. The Lord gave me a totally new insight about my life, people in my life and my journey. I believe He was showing me how these trees represented life, in general.

I heard, "It is necessary for the trees to shed their leaves because they shed off all the things that are old and worn out; and they are able to breathe and rejuvenate. So when the new leaves come back, they are restored and ready for the next few seasons to weather the storms....*and* to provide shade!" I believe these trees are a representation of a divine relationship with the Heavenly Father. A season of shedding is necessary. The Lord sheds me of heart ache, disappointment, negativity, negative people, frustration, doubt, anger, fear, etc. He strips it all from me, so I can breathe. Then, I am restored with new grace; and refreshed with stronger faith in Him, strength, mercy, determination, endurance, love stewardship, and a more matured spirit and mind set. Hallelujah!

Then I heard, "You see, the other tree does not shed so that it can be rejuvenated. It *looks* like it is the strongest because of the durability of the leaves. A few leaves may dry up and fall off, but for the most part it carries the same old leaves year after year. Nothing ever changes about it." Well, there are some people like that, as well. They never accept adaptation to change in their lives. They do the same thing year after year and there is never any growth. I am not only talking about money, materialistic and superficial things; but I am talking about spiritual growth as well. They have been imprisoned by religion and restricted to an *inside of the box* thought pattern and lifestyle. Their lives may look like they have it all together because of the healthy salary they have acquired or the luxury home they live in; or maybe even the exotic car they drive or the title they wear in front of their name. But, deep down on the inside nothing has changed. They have the same old drama, still treating people like crap, but fronting in the public's eye like they are so holy. They are cheating and deceiving people yet proclaiming that they love the Lord. You know what I am talking about.... Same *old* leaves. Come on now.... I must tell the truth! Someone will get mad and offended about what I just said, but all I will say is that sometimes the truth hurts, yet it is definitely healing!

So, you know I quickly changed my mind about wanting to be like the tree that never sheds; because it hardly ever gets to experience new leaves! It is necessary to go thru the process the Lord has instructed for us. Everyone is not the same, nor is their situations and circumstances. This journey that I have been on for a while has taught me not to be so quick to judge and make assumptions about people and their circumstances; because their journey just may be purposed for them, in that particular season of their life, for spiritual growth and for God's Glory.

I used to think that the winter season was the worst because of the trials that would always come along. But just as I was writing this chapter, the Lord showed me that trials will always come; and the *winter* season was not the worst; yet, it was the time to recognize and appreciate how His amazing grace had sustained me! In my perception, it symbolizes the Lord's divine covering He has over my life. Wow! What a revelation! My *winter* season was also the time for me to reflect on the greatness of the Lord, to rest, to rejuvenate and to prepare!

If you are in the *winter* season of your life, embrace it with thanksgiving and know it is not a time to be down and out, yet on the contrary, it is a time to praise and prepare for all the greater blessings that He has waiting just for you. Your *winter* season is not the time to throw in the towel because it appears nothing is happening for you; yet, it is the time to prepare for what has already manifested for you in His realm! He is waiting patiently for you to get there! We thank you, Lord God, for ALL the new seasons to come, in Jesus name. Amen. 2 Corinthians 5:17

~~~~~~

Great Challenges, Great Faith,
Great Deliverance, Great Blessings,
GREATEST GOD!

~~~~~~

WATCH THIS!

Watch this! Look very
closely. It is all plain to see
To see how I am bringing you out of the
storm and lifting you out of the valley

I chose you as my servant so you may
know and understand who I truly am
I chose you so you would learn that
my powers are not a spiritual scam

Watch this! Look very closely so
you may clearly see my lowliness
I chose you that I may cleanse your soul
and, you too, may walk in my Holiness

I chose you so you may know I am
God and, about your life, I do care
I chose you as one of my vessels that I
may use to fight this spiritual warfare

Watch this! Look very closely. You
can clearly see that my spirit is serene
I purposely brought you into my presence
so I may create, in you, a brand new thing

I chose you to go thru your tests and trials
because I equipped you to handle it
I knew you would bare the fiery flames
and not turn around and run, give up or quit

Watch this! Look very closely. You can see
the blessings I give with one stroke of my hand
I told you I would make a way in the
desert and streams in the wastelands

I chose you because I knew, for me, you
would have the courage to stand and fight
I knew you would trust that I would be there for
you, even if I was not in your physical eye sight

Watch this! Look very closely. You can
see that I am safely sheltering you
Because of your obedience, I will pour out the
treasures of Heaven like the sweet morning dew

I chose you, my child, because I desired to
save you from the world, yourself and sinning
And I want you to know the blessings you are
receiving are only a taste of the beginning

April 26, 2011
Isaiah 43:18-19

CHAPTER 6

THE *EVICTION* PROCESS

It was Tuesday, July 18, 2017 and I was sitting at my dining room table urgently seeking direction from the Lord. I was told three days before my rent, for June, was due that the income I had worked for was depleted; and my pay check would only be forty-six dollars. I sat in silence and disbelief. I had been evicted from my apartment and it was the 8th day since the Writ of Possession had been filed. We were supposed to be out of the apartment by July 10th, but I had no money to move or even to rent a storage unit for my belongings. The manager of the complex had come by to see if I had vacated the apartment; and when I had opened the door, she looked baffled as to why I was still there. She asked when I was leaving and I, respectfully, told her I did not know. She then got an attitude with me and walked away.

In addition to the eviction, the dealership I had purchased my car thru had called to inform me that they were coming to repossess it. The lady who spoke with me was extremely rude and insensitive which I politely brought to her attention. Everything was due, and I did not have a clue as to how I was going to pay it all. My children were helping me to stay afloat with the utilities. I thank God for my wonderful children because they are always there in the good times and in the challenging times of my life! So after I hung up with the rude lady, I went to my room, closed the door and continued to pray for direction. I did not know what I was going to do, but I refused to give up on God. My biggest concern was my god son who had come to live with me at the beginning of the year.

I asked him if he wanted to go back to our home town with his other family because of everything that I was going thru, at the time; and he insisted that he stay with me. I expressed to him that this journey would not be a piece of cake and, yet, he still insisted on staying. I prayed about it and the Lord moved, in me, to keep him here with me. I was very nervous because all of my children were grown, and I could have easily figured out a way to manage if it were just me. But, I had a minor child with me and I could not let him down. He did not want to go back to where he had come from and I did not want him to go back. Thinking of him and the situation I was in caused the days to become very stressful; because I could not grasp an understanding as to why I had to keep going thru when I have worked so hard, all the time, to support my family. I just could not wrap my mind around the situation. I was disappointed and frustrated because I did not quit my job....it had suddenly quit me....no warnings whatsoever.

The one person I thought I could depend on, to pray for me and speak encouragement, tore my heart to pieces when she said what I thought would never come out of her mouth because she was such a God-fearing woman. When I respectfully told her that I would not be able to fulfill my obligation that was coming up because of my unforeseen circumstances, she had become very upset with me and said, "I don't know what it is, Rayna, but you got to be doing something wrong. I mean....I get in a bind sometimes, but you are always in a bind." Then she proceeded to say, "I do not have any money so you're just going to have to come and sit down so we can talk because you got to be doing something wrong." Lord, have mercy! My heart hit the ground after I had hung up the phone with her. I broke down into crocodile tears because I thought, "Here's a godly woman—who had been knowing me for over seven years and knows how hard I work to provide for my family—telling me that I have got to be doing something wrong." If I was not rooted in my Heavenly Father, I would have possibly believed what she had said to me; because I would always listen to her wisdom. But this time, she was dead wrong. First of all, I never even told her my situation when I had called her; nor have I ever asked her for any money. I would always work for it. There were times when she blessed me "just because" and I am truly grateful for that. But to hear someone that I truly admired say such negative words, to me, was extremely heartbreaking. What God had allowed me to realize is that this was not just the *Eviction Notice* for my home, but it was an eviction notice for some people in my life, as well.

Sometimes, God have to remove people out of our circle while we are going thru certain journeys in our life. Most people will not understand our assignment because it is not of the *norm*, and because they have never experienced what we have gone thru and where the Lord is taking us to, in this season. They are so stuck on religion and tradition that they cannot see how the power of God is so much greater than what we have experienced, thus far.

God is doing a brand new thing in this land, and if you are not open to receiving it, you will drastically miss it. Just because people do not understand your journey does not mean, for one moment, that you have done something wrong! It is, simply, the Lord stretching your faith in order to launch you into what HE has purposed for you which is much more than your mind could ever conceive; if you only believe!

You see, this is my life's journey….my extraordinary assignment He has chosen for me to fulfill. Everyone's journey is not the same. My ministry is Faith and God has purposed and created me just for this faith assignment; and He has given me everything I need to achieve and conquer it….HIMSELF! At times, I cry, I get frustrated, I want to give up and I get upset with God. Yet, He ALWAYS comes to remind me of His grace, by Faith, that will carry me thru on every assignment. He sends His Holy Spirit to encamp me with His provisions, protection and His reassurance that everything WILL be alright thru the process! If you have lurking individuals who are speaking negativity in your ear, please do yourself a favor and EVICT them, RIGHT NOW!!! Some evictions will be seasonal and others for a lifetime. God wants to do a new thing in your life and it will be more challenging to move forward when you have negative voices whispering doubt into your spirit.

Another week had gone by and, by God's precious grace and mercy; we were still in the apartment. I had been doing all I could to figure out a way to acquire income and another home for my family. Nothing was happening; at least that is what I had felt, at the time. I was saving what little bit of money I had for when we had to leave the apartment. After surrendering my issue to the Lord, His Holy Spirit caused me to rebuke stress, frustration, fear and worry, thru the process. He gave me the strength to continue with faith, in Him, and to keep pressing forward. It was manifested in my spirit that no matter what happened I would trust the Lord with ALL my heart and soul.

And finally, the day had come when my faith, in the Lord, would be tested. Everything He had been preparing me for, thru His Word and in time of meditation, was about to be tried.... Psalm 27:5-10

When I Surrendered

God, I gave my life completely
over to you in Jesus name
And it seems as though when I surrendered
that's when my most challenging trials came

I thought you told me I was more than
a conqueror and I would not be defeated
Now I'm sitting here basically homeless
and all of my funds have been depleted

I thought you told me that I
would stand firm and be victorious
But there's nothing about these heartaches
and pains that make this life feel glorious

I thought you told me to be of good cheer
because, with you, the battle is already won
So why am I pacing the floor night and day
wondering where our next meal will come from

I thought you told me you would wipe
away the tears when, from these eyes, I cry
So why do I continue to hear the same
response; denied, denied, denied

I thought you told me that if I rebuke the enemy in
Jesus name; he would have to flee without a doubt
So why am I being lied on, laughed
at, ridiculed and talked about

I thought you told me you would give me the desires
of my heart and if I knocked the doors would be opened
So why do I feel all alone in these storms looking
for a way out; and barely even coping

Then you said to me, "Look at yourself
in the mirror; you are still standing
I have taught you how to become humble
and not so aggressive and demanding

I have taught you to have faith in what
you cannot see and in the unknown
I have taught you to believe in the impossible
now look how much your faith has grown

I have taught you patience because I needed
you to learn how to be still and wait on me
I never told you this would be a
comfortable or even a simple journey

I have taught you how to endure
so you may stand the test of time
And yes, I did say the battle was won
because victory will always be mine

I have taught you how to communicate
with me, thru supplication, when you pray
You have learned what I tell you *is*
for you and not what the world says

You have learned how to let go of the heartaches
and disappointment and how to forgive
You have learned how to reject schemes of
the enemy so in peace and joy you may live

I knew you would endure these trials because
I am the One who has your destiny planned out
You've surrendered and have overcome, so
tell me child, what are you complaining about

I chose you as my anointed one and
you have finally answered the call
I know you can see for yourself
that it was not a mistake at all

You are a witness that my love and protection
is truly merciful, sweet and oh so tender
And now you are ready to minister to others, the glory
of God, in Jesus name, when it is their turn to surrender."

May 20, 2014
Isaiah 64:8

God is so much bigger than our trials, circumstances and any challenge that comes our way! They are but the dust under His feet!

Chapter 7

The Writ Executed

It was July 31, 2017 when the Sheriff Department had entered my home to evict us from the apartment. My daughter, grandchildren, god son and I were there. It took every bit of what little strength I had left to keep from dropping tears. I quickly gained my composure and told my daughter to take the children to the park that was in the complex. The officer asked if I had a truck coming to load my belongings and I sadly told him no. He looked at me with confusion and dismay in his eyes as he asked what I was going to do with all of it. With brokenness in my heart, I humbly told him that I was going to leave it all. Once the children had left, I grabbed what I could and exited the apartment only to see about ten to twelve guys waiting on my steps to come in and set my belongings outside in one of the complex parking spaces. I thank God for my daughter because she was right there with me thru what was such a humiliating moment of my life. I insisted that she stay at the park with the children and she refused. She said, "Momma, I'm not leaving you." And the one person who I was praying would not be there to see this happen to me, was there.

My neighbor who lived in front of me was not fond of me and vice versa. Our spirits did not connect, at all, so I kept my distance. I would always politely speak but I would not take it any further than that. When she saw what was happening to me, this heartless woman had a smirk on her face as if my misfortune was humorous to her. She was laughing with the management staff; and she kept walking back and forth to her vehicle, which just so happened to be parked close to my car, looking over at me with that same devilish smirk on her face. I cannot lie to you…. I was about to walk over there to curse her out and stomp her face into the ground, but my daughter grabbed me and said, "No momma, she's not even worth it. She'll see you again and next time it won't be this way." I stopped in my tracks and realized what she had said to me. I began to calm down and continued loading my trunk. I began to praise the Lord right on thru the humiliation; and my baby girl was right there with me. I am so grateful that she insisted on staying with me because, to be honest, I would have probably gone to jail for punching my neighbor in the face. Hey, do not judge me! I am not perfect.... I am just being honest! We all have limitations and breaking points. Thank God for grace and intercession! After I filled the car with as much of our belongings as I could, I told my daughter to get in the car. We picked the children up from the park and drove away from it all.

I was confused as to why God would allow my neighbor to be there, to see what happened to me, when she was NEVER there at that particular time. I prayed about it, and for her, as well. Most of the time, the challenges we go thru is only partly for us; and the other part is for someone else. At that moment, it felt as though it was the worst thing to go thru; and I could not even see how I was going to bounce back from it. I felt like I was at my wits end with everything that had happened.

It is in the moments like the one I had when you should reflect on all the previous trials the Lord has brought you thru. And when you reflect on His love and faithfulness, gratefulness fills your heart which drives you to praise. And when you praise, you find yourself filled with divine strength to keep on pushing. It is the Holy Spirit on the inside of you that will not let you give up. It wills you to keep going....to keep pressing your way thru. And thoughts like, "Tomorrow could be the day for my breakthrough," is what keeps you hanging on.

After I finished praying for the young lady, the Lord ministered to me that, yes, she will see me again and that same incident she laughed at would be the same incident that ministers to her spirit. Hallelujah, thank you Lord God!

Sometimes we cannot see what the Lord has planned ahead for us. At times, it seems and feels like failure when really, He has positioned us for unusual and favorable prosperity. I could not understand why He allowed this to happen when I only had two months left on my lease. But as I sulked in my tears, He made me realize that my timing was not His timing; and He knew what was best for me. Yes, this experience was one heck of a challenge for me, but I thank God for the challenge; because He allowed me to execute my Faith He had manifested within me. I would have never known I could make it thru if my faith was not put to the test. God is an awesome and remarkable God and there was no way He was going to leave me and my family...ABSOLUTELY NO WAY!

Did I desire to be in that hotel? I did not! That was God's will for my life and, by His grace, I accepted it and fulfilled His purpose which has been destined for me in that season of my life. I could have written this book in my car, as I did with the first book, so I did not complain. I am sure He knew what was best for me; and HE is the ONLY one that I TRUSTED wholeheartedly.

Trust God no matter what and allow Him to do a good work in you. It may hurt, sometimes, but if you give it all over to Him—which sometimes is easier said than done—He will be the comforter of your spirit; and you will be surprised how He will fill you with peace, joy and strength you so desire right in the midst of the storm. He is just that sovereign and compassionate. He is God and God all by Himself, in Jesus name. Amen. Philippians 1:6

~~~~~~

Manifestation is a result of who or what we put our Faith in; whether positive or negative. Learning to speak with wisdom and discernment, along with faith and obedience, is essential to positive manifestation

~~~~~~

SET FREE

I have been strapped down
and bound in chains for so long
I did not think I had the
strength to continue on

I was held hostage in my
spirit and I desired to be free
I was ready for a divine
intervention; ready to be released

Released from the world and
its deceitful imprisonment
So I may gain true kingdom
wisdom and spiritual discernment

Released from this life of
hate and perverse thoughts
Knowing that God stills loves
me beyond my worldly flaws

Released from the things
I thought made me whole
Released from idol gods
and the lies I was told

Released from deception
that is carried out by night
Knowing what is done in
the dark will come to the light

I need to be released; my
life is rapidly falling apart
I need someone greater than the
world to restore, in me, a new heart

Wash me, cleanse me and make me
whole again; oh how I desire to be free
I am down on my knees in tears
requesting, Lord, that you please release me

Release me, please, release
me; I desire to be free again
I desire to be delivered by the
Master while I'm in this land

No longer do I desire to accept
what the world has to give
I desire to be saved and delivered; so
in the Father's Will, I shall forever live

November 26, 2011
Romans 6:18

Chapter 8

Protection Thru The Process

When the Lord God has called us into our purpose, He has not only made provisions for us to fulfill the purpose, but He has also provided us with His protection, as well. Walking in the Will of God is a very narrow path; and while on that path, there will be times when we will become nervous and even afraid. The enemy will try to tempt us with fear. He will use people who will try to intimidate us, but, remember if God brought us to it, He will, without a doubt, protect us while we go thru it. He will send protection in ways we never expect.

As I was praying for protection, over my family and I while staying here in this hotel, the Lord reminded me of a time back in 2009 when I had lost my home, the first time, due to some challenging circumstances. My children and I had to move to a place that was far from their school. My finances were limited so I sat in the park, each day, and waited for their school day to end. While going thru my experience in the park, I would always pray for protection. I remember being nervous the first week I was out there because, sometimes, I would fall asleep in the car. The Lord had calmed my spirit and I felt reassured that He had covered me. I went about my days in peace and comfort because of His loving spirit that surrounded me.

One morning, in the second week at the park, there was this police officer who had driven by and stared at me as if I was out there to get into mischief. When he drove pass me to exit the park, I stared at him to assure him that I was not trouble. Every day that I was in the park, the same police officer would drive pass me, once in the early morning and once in mid-afternoon. We would always make eye contact when he entered the park. We never said one word to each other....at least not from our mouth. I knew the officer was heaven sent. God had sent him to watch over and protect me.

One day, around early noon, there was an older man driving a late model pickup truck who had come into the park. As he slowly drove pass me, he stared at me with a look of perversion in his eyes. I rolled my eyes at him and kept writing. Next thing I know, he had returned to where I was parked and reversed his truck into the space next to my car. Of course, being who I am, I pulled my crowbar from under my seat and I began to pray to the Lord with urgency in my heart. I said, "Lord God, you know your daughter will use this crowbar if this man comes over to my car. You told me that you were going to protect me." By this time, the officer had already made his morning round; and it would be another hour and a half before he made his afternoon round. Well, the perverted man got out of his truck and portrayed like he was checking his tires while his eyes were locked in on me. He had come around to the side of his truck where I was parked so I grabbed my crowbar from the floor and held on to it tightly. He had bent down to look at his tire and when he rose up, it was to my amazement that I saw the officer coming down the drive!

The officer had come earlier than usual! And when he drove pass me, we made visual contact. I stared at him with distress in my eyes. He would usually drive to the back of the park and sit for a while and then drive back up; oh, but not that particular day! He turned around and drove right back up and reversed his police car into the space that was directly across from me. I did not take my eyes off him. He stared at the perverted man and did not take his eyes off of him! The man became very nervous. He portrayed that he was looking at his head light. He walked back to the driver side of his truck, jumped in and drove off quickly! The officer turned his focus back to me. He stayed right there for about five minutes and he did not take his eyes off me! I finally calmed down and I believe he saw a sense of relief in my eyes, because he slowly drove away towards the exit of the park. Tears of gratefulness began to stream down my face.

The Lord kept His promise to me! He sent His protection to keep me covered. I do not know and will probably never know what happened that caused the officer to make his afternoon round early on that day. But rest assured, there is one thing I do know....it was the Heavenly Father who sent him! He is the Faithful God! He keeps us in ways that we cannot ever imagine. I called on Him and He answered me, quickly. He knew that I did not want to cause harm to anyone, nor did I want harm to come upon me, so He fixed it just as He said he would—right in the nick of time!

God's grace is sufficient for all of us. He will never leave or forsake us because He loves us so much. If you are in a moment when you feel nervous and afraid, call on the Lord and KNOW that He WILL come to your rescue, in Jesus name. Amen. Psalm 20:1-2

~~~~~~~~~~~~~~~~~~~~~~~~~~
Not "somehow", yet, "GOD IS HOW"!
~~~~~~~~~~~~~~~~~~~~~~~~~~

I'VE BEEN KEPT

Part II

I've been kept thru the
embarrassment and thru the shame
Been kept by my Father's
mercy thru Jesus' name

I've been kept thru the
rumors and deceitful lies
Been kept thru the disappointment
and the tears I've cried

I've been kept thru my
faults, disobedience and sin
Been kept when I thought I had
lost and then knew I would win

I've been kept when I
wanted to lie down and die
Been kept when I wanted
to give up and not even try

I've been kept when I chose
to walk this journey of faith
Been kept when I felt, from
others, less love and more hate

I've been kept when I was talked
about, ridiculed and criticized
Been kept when it was said that
my decisions were not wise

I've been kept when I was given
assignments I did not understand
Been kept when I felt alone but then
knew He was holding my hand

I've been kept when satan
tried to play tricks with my mind
Been kept when God have
blocked his schemes every time

I've been kept when I
did not have much at all
Been kept thru Jesus Christ
when on His name I called

I've been kept when I was
weak and did not want to stand
Been kept by the voice of
my Father's command

I've been kept when I felt my
life was being torn and tossed
Been kept by my Savior, oh thank
you, Lord Jesus, for paying the cost

January 4, 2012
Psalm 23

Chapter 9

It Only Looks Broken

God replayed a memory, in my mind, of one morning when I was led to return to my pillar in the park that I use to go to, previously, in 2009. I returned to reflect and worship the Lord for how great he had been to me and my family. I remember when I first had to sit in the park; I had lost my job and my home. At the time, I had a 1992 Buick Regal that was wrecked, but it still ran decent and the heat worked very well. I would have to leave the place where we were staying, at the time, around 6am to drop my children off at school by 7am and drop my grandson off at daycare; and if either one of them had become sick, they had to stay in the car with me because I could not afford to drive back to where we were dwelling and then return to pick them up each day. After I dropped my babies off, I would go to the park to begin my day.

First, I would meditate on the Lord and God would allow poetic words to flow from my spirit as I cried; and even when I was angry about my situation, I continued to write what I heard. When I finished meditating, I would get the phone book out of the trunk and call doctors' offices to get their fax numbers so my resume could be faxed to them. This was before emails and online applications became so popular. I had a friend who would fax my resume to most of the numbers that I had compiled each day. I am truly grateful for what she had done. I also went to the library to wait for my children and to apply for jobs. And when I had an interview, I would bring my clothes with me and get dressed in my storage unit if the library was not open. This happened for about two months. But, there was one specific thing about this journey that I believe I will not ever forget—EVER.

I would always back into the same parking space, in the park that faced these two broken trees that were next to each other. For some reason, the Lord always moved in me to focus on these two trees. They were almost a stub. I would often hear, "stay focused on the broken trees." I never understood, in those moments, why I had to focus on the brokenness of these two trees, but I was obedient to His instruction. Every time I went to the park, I made time to focus on those particular trees, while I continued to search for employment and write poetry. So, after three months had passed and I was finally hired for a job, which had received my resume two years prior, I left the park still not understanding why I had to focus on the two broken trees. It was not until the 24th day of January 2017, when I returned to the park to reflect, that the Lord had finally given me revelation about those two amazing trees. He will use anything to minister His glory, power, faithfulness and sovereignty to us!

When I was sitting in the park reflecting over His faithfulness to me, and how He blessed me to publish the book of poetry in 2011 that I had written in the car; He brought to my memory the broken trees. I began to look for them, but they were nowhere to be found! I knew I was looking in the right place. After eight years, those two trees had grown back just as tall and strong as the other trees. It was like they had never been broken at all! I heard, as I was staring at them in amazement, "You have weathered the storm." I must pause for a moment to say, "Thank You Lord God!" The Lord continues to carry me thru it all and I am truly grateful. Next, I heard, "Never forget this place and where you have come from. Always have compassion for others who go thru trials and challenges." I received all of it, in the name of Jesus!

There is this old saying that goes "I may bend but I won't break". But after that day of seeing those broken trees restored, the Lord totally showed me otherwise! I was shown, YES, we can break and sometimes we will, but as long as we are connected to the *ROOT*, we WILL NOT DIE! We WILL grow to be bigger and better than what we have ever been before!

At times, we have to be broken. We need be purified from bad habits and worldly thoughts. We must be broken from the deceptive belief system that we were born into. I know the Lord had to break me of some unrighteous ways I had possessed. He broke me from drug habits, lying, cheating, insecurities, low self-esteem and self-doubt. He broke me from worry and fear! The process was hectic, but I humbly chose to surrender my ALL to Him, anyhow. I continued with faith in Him no matter how hectic the journey had become. I chose to stay rooted, in my Father, no matter how much I was told my decisions were unheard of and how impossible they were. I chose to stay rooted, in Him, even when I knew that I could make quick money to sustain me and my family and live an "easy" life. I thank God for the ROOTS! You see, as long as those two trees were connected to the ROOTS, they were still ALIVE! They only *appeared* to be broken—they only *looked* dead to the physical eye.

The world has deceived many of you by creating an illusion that what you see on the outside is what gives life to your soul. I used to be one who was deceived. It has convinced you that if you do not have a certain level of education, you are not intelligent; and if you are not in a certain position, you are not important. The world uses the media and "so called" statistics to convince you that your gifts are obsolete; and you allow them to unconsciously mold your mind into the path they have chosen for you. It uses money, fancy cars and homes, name brand clothes and shoes, purses, expensive vacations, etc. to convince you that these materialistic things are what define who you are; and if you do not have them, your life is not prosperous. Why? Because, you did not follow the "world's" strategic plan for your life, therefore, you are not a valuable asset to anyone or anything. The world endorses perversion by plastering it in our children's schools, in the media and even in some churches to persuade you into thinking that just because it is your life you can do whatever you choose to do…like there will be no consequences behind the decisions you make. Oh but, my Heavenly Father has brought me to the forefront to boldly contradict all of this nonsense!

I am a witness that as long as you are connected to the ROOT, you are still ALIVE! The life of the tree does not come from what we physically see; yet on the contrary, it comes from the *source* that is planted deep into the earth which is not visible—the ROOTS which are watered from the rains and nurtured by the sunshine! If you are not connected to Him, I urge you to get connected. There will be days where you will experience pain, disappointment, discouragement, sadness, abandonment, loneliness and hurt. But I can tell you from my own personal journey that all of those feelings are only GROWING PAINS, if you allow them to be! Please do not allow anyone to convince you otherwise; and trust me, they will try.

At times, people who are the closest to you will give up on you before anyone else; but do not fret about that because those are the people who are not meant to continue with you in the season of your journey. Most of the time, it will be the people you would least expect such as your "traditional" family and friends. Those are the very people who still keep God in a box. They are the first to say, "Baby, nothing is too hard for God!" "He can do anything." But when the time comes for the *anything* to happen, they think you have lost your everlasting mind and have done something wrong, all because you are on a journey that they do not understand and have never experienced for themselves. KEEP GOING, I SAY!! You are on the righteous path of the Heavenly Father—the Narrow Path!

When you are being restored (humbled), back to God from brokenness, it can hurt, sometimes. You have to be stretched (tested), you have to endure (patience) and you have to fight thru the pain (persevere) to get to the point where you can praise (be grateful), even thru the storms. In the words of Pastor Eugene "G" Whitmore, "The Lord knows that you can do whatever it is He has called you to do because He created you, yet you go thru challenges and trials so *you* may know for yourself (confidence) that *you* are able to do what He has called you to do." I believe when He takes us into our destiny He has chosen for us, there can be absolutely no doubt, in our mind, when He moves in us and gives us instruction. There has to be a genuine TRUST in His spirit and in His will; because what He has purposed for us is not just for our own lives, but for many other lives who feel that they are only "existing" in this land. Our ministry does not begin when we are restored; yet on the contrary, I believe it begins when we are broken!

You have to remember that when you feel or even look broken, YOU ARE NOT DEAD! As long as you are connected to the ROOT of life—which is our Lord and Savior Jesus Christ—you WILL live to the maximum potential He has purposed for you, if you believe! I am not saying that materialistic blessings are a curse or that we should not have and enjoy them; but what I am ministering to you is when you keep your focus on the SOURCE and walk in His Will, then, HE will give you ALL of these blessings in abundance; because He desires for his children to live in royalty and in victory. His word says so! NEVER allow anyone to convince you that your life does not matter or that it is over for you. And no matter what you go thru, PLEASE remember to always stay connected to the divine root. The ROOT is where the nourishments will come from that will cause you to grow stronger and better than what you were before! YOU ARE A WINNER, in Jesus name. Amen. Matthew 6:33; John 15:1-17; 3 John 1:2

There are rain showers that saturate only the surface. And there are rain storms that saturate the roots!

NATURE

The purity of your spirit rests upon
my soul like the sweet morning dew
Just can't fathom why anyone would
reject the opportunity of worshipping you

Your joy fills this vessel as the
rays of the noon day sunshine
No matter how hard the world tries to
consume me, your joy out shines it every time

Your peace is as calming as a
river flowing gently downstream
It reminds me that the trials in my
life aren't really as bad as they seem

Your grace surpasses the altitude
of the highest point of the mountains
It is so freely poured out on me
as a continuous flowing fountain

Your mercy is sustaining as the
smallest tree blown by aggressive winds
When the world thought I was broken
you were building me up from within

Your sovereignty excels pass any
king who sits on their earthly throne
It doesn't take an army to win the battle
it's won by the power of your voice alone

Your wisdom is as the darkest hour of the
evening consumed by the array of moonlight
It empowers my feeble mind
with divine knowledge and insight

Your discernment is as the star that
directs my path when I have lost my way
It instructs me when to be silent, how
to react and the words I should say

Your blessings are as many as the rain
showers when, to the earth, they fall
When you send them to me from
Heaven, I just can't count them all

Your forgiveness is as the grains of
dirt washed away by the winds and rain
You have placed all of my sins behind
you and never again shall they remain

Lord, your love is more beautiful than
the most exquisite botanical of gardens
You gave up your only son as
a ransom and for my pardon

Your intimacy is like walking on the
greenest grass that filters between my toes
You're my best friend whom I can confide
in and trust with my heart the most

Thank you for the favor you have given
to me while I'm still here on this earth
Thank you for teaching me and allowing
me to know my heavenly worth

You've saved me from the guilt stains,
my worldly ways and corrupt behavior
And you've manifested, within me, your
Loving kindness, your Holy Spirit
and your very own divine nature

May 15, 2014
Psalm 46:4-5

Chapter 10

The *Limbo* Period

Have you ever been in a moment, in life, where you just did not know which way to turn or what decision to make? It seems like, no matter what you did to make progression in your life, you feel as though you had fallen ten steps backwards. Have you ever felt like the love you have poured out into the people you truly value was poured out in vane? Well if you have, then you understand how I had felt in such moments. It was October 18, 2017 and I was sitting, at the hotel table listening to Tasha Cobbs Leonard "Forever at Your Feet", not knowing which way to go. It seemed as though nothing was moving in my favor. But the strength I had on the inside would not allow me to give up. It kept tugging at me to keep going, no matter what.

There was a pregnant lady with two children who stayed in the room beside us; and she allowed her children to scream and beat on the table and walls. I tried so hard to concentrate on writing this book, but, most of the time I was distracted by all the drama that was going on. My focus began to fade, and my mind traveled back to my situation. I tried to focus on something that would keep me motivated and encouraged, but at times, it just did not go as planned. The stress of my situation and other personal family issues brought me to tears that today. But no matter how much and how hard I cried, my spirit kept trusting and praising the Lord. I refused to give up because I AM NOT A QUITTER. I am more than a CONQUEROR!

At times, we will have to walk a journey that we do not understand—a FAITH journey; but remember that most of the journeys that God allows us to experience is not just for us; because our lives are not our own. We—the children of God who has an intimate relationship with Him—are surrendered vessels for the Lord to implement His mighty works thru us so others who are lost and confused can be drawn into Him and be saved, by His amazing grace.

This particular journey was one of the most challenging journeys I had experienced, but my Heavenly Father was in control of my life. I have and will always welcome Him to have control; because I know when I put all of my cares in His hands, EVERYTHING is going to be alright. I have always been protected and provided for thru the journeys He had allowed me to experience. He had already made the way for me. I praise the name of the Lord God! I knew the truth was He will NEVER leave or forsake me. I knew that even though I cried, He was right there to comfort me. I knew while I was in *Limbo*, it had already been worked out before He even brought me to that point. Oh yes, I knew that when I did not know which way to go or what decision to make, He had already planted my feet in His righteous direction. Faith in Him is what God desired of me and of you, as well.

Confidence in the Lord is what He desires for you to have. He welcomes it! It gives Him the opportunity to show you more of Himself in your circumstances and challenges. He is waiting to do far more for you than you give Him credit for. He is NOT a mediocre God! He is the GREAT AND MIGHTY CREATER who desires to perform supernatural blessings for you and for others to see as well!

He desires to do for you what the world tells you, each and every day, cannot be done. He desires to use you for His glory! And it pleasures the Lord to bless His children just as it pleasures you, as a parent, to bless your children He has gifted to you. Know that when you are in *Limbo*, it is a time to praise the Lord for what has already taken place for His glory and for the benefit of your future! Praise causes the Lord to shift you into the manifestation of the blessings He has waiting just for you. A grateful heart pleases the Lord! It is also a time to allow Him to fill you with His comfort, strength and wisdom. It is a time to PREPARE!

At times, even a person with an intimate relationship with the Lord feels like giving up. There are moments where the journey can get so intense that it brings you to a point of wanting to throw in the towel. You began to question the Father. You have walked in obedience to Him, you have trusted and kept the Faith, you have prayed for others and have watched their blessings come to pass. And here you are still waiting, still hoping, still praying, still walking in obedience, still trusting the Father; and yet, the trials continue to pour out like a flood, in your life. You break down in tears and you ask the Heavenly Father when will your turn come to get a blessing and relief in your life?

You are not in the streets partying and living a wild life; you take care of your family, you give to others, you pray, praise and worship Him yet it still seems as though nothing is happening for you. You throw your hands up and say, "Lord, whatever.... whatever YOU want." It is like you have given up to a certain extent. Well, to be honest, you really have not given up; instead, you have given in!

You are not strong enough, in your own will, to handle the trials and challenges that come your way. And when you begin to focus on those distractions—because that is exactly what they are—the stress of the world seems to become overwhelmingly heavy upon you which makes you feel like you cannot go on. But in actuality, you have taken your focus off of the Heavenly Father and His deity. You see, your complete help comes from the Lord; because the word says that "the joy of the Lord is our strength." God's strength is manifested within you, by His grace. But when you take your focus off of Him, you begin to operate in your flesh. You become weak and in distress; which is what I had done on that particular day. God allows trials and tests to come in your life in order to strengthen you (mature you spiritually) for what He has purposed for you and for your destiny.

Walking the narrow path will have its challenges. If you are genuinely honest with yourself, you can admit that tears have been and will be shed, frustration comes upon you, discouragement knocks at the door of your heart and soul, disappointment creeps up on you and doubt, sometimes, fill your mind. Walking the narrow path in faith, for the Heavenly Father to get the glory, is much easier said than done. It takes a genuine desire, practice, dedication, commitment, endurance, perseverance and most of all it takes God's love, grace, mercy and His almighty strength. God's strength gives you the *supernatural will* to, faithfully, keep pressing forward when everything on the inside of you indicates that you just cannot go any farther. This is why it is imperative for the children of the Most High God to stay connected to Him, in spirit and in truth. So whenever you feel like calling it quits, think of the broken trees! Please do not give up; yet, only *give in* to the Source who will empower you, supernaturally, to keep pressing toward your purpose.

Lord, no matter how we—your children—feel right now, here we are. Use us the way You choose; because we know that we will be used the righteous way…. YOUR way. We know our lives will have increase with You. Increase in our faith, wisdom and discernment, our finances, our health and strength, and most of all, our hearts, spirit and love. Thank you for the journey, Lord. We know that you are not just with us; yet, you are *in* us and for that we are grateful, in Jesus name. Amen. Hebrews 13:6; 2Corinthians 12:9; Nehemiah 8:10

The God of Your Word

Lord, I know you to be the
gracious God of your word
I believe what you have
shown me and what I have heard

You said your word would never
come back to you empty or void
Therefore, when it returns to you
it is fulfilled and never destroyed

When you give a command, your
Holy Will must come to pass
Even if it is not understood because
your wisdom, no one can surpass

If you say that I have to do it
then it must be, faithfully, done
Trusting in you, Lord, that victory
is yours and I have already won

Lord, I am your vessel who is here to
do your will; my position is to serve
Because you are first and foremost
in my life; not second or third

God, your faithfulness and love you
so freely give to me, I do not deserve
But my spirit is humble and I am truly
grateful that you are the God of your Word

April 21, 2011
Isaiah 55:8-11

~~~~~~~~~~~~~~~~~~~~~~~~~

*Giving God praise thru the
challenges is truly a stress reliever!*

~~~~~~~~~~~~~~~~~~~~~~~~~

Chapter 11

Comfort In The Crying Times

The tears will not stop flowing no matter how hard you try to conceal them. Any little negative thing triggers your emotions and, once again, you are crying your eyes out. Your struggle has gotten you tangled in so much stress and frustration; and it feels as though you are drowning in your sorrows. You are begging for God to give you some relief, but it seems as though He is not listening to you; and it seems as though He has turned his back on you. You call your closest friend hoping to get answers as to why you are going thru such challenging trials, but no answer he or she gives consoles your aching heart. You go to your pastor, but no matter how much he or she prays for you, you just cannot find peace in your spirit. You feel like you are about to have a nervous breakdown and there is no one there to help you. You feel like the walls are caving in on you by the second. I am here to tell you that I have definitely experienced that feeling; and even though you feel the Lord has left you, understand that He could never leave you because He is *IN* you!

Three weeks had passed since my family and I had been in the hotel room. I had already been feeling down and out about my challenging situation when I nearly had a nervous breakdown, in my car. I had just finished grocery shopping, and had put the groceries in the trunk, when I realized that my cell phone was not in my pocket. I had placed it there as I walked into the store because I did not have my purse with me. When I started the car to head back to the room, I reached for my phone and it was not there. I had already had some emotional moments earlier; and losing my phone was all I needed to take me over the edge. My heart began to pound as I got out of the car to look under the seat and in the trunk where I had put the groceries….no phone. I went back to the cart station to see if I left it in the cart….no phone. So

I walked back to the car, got in, slammed the door and drove off. I was eating a Snickers ice cream bar and, as I drove off the lot, I broke down. Tears began to stream down my face, profusely. I could barely see the road. I slung my ice cream bar out of the window and began to beat on the steering wheel. I was screaming like I had lost my everlasting mind.... well, at the time, I really felt that I was on the verge of going crazy. I was extremely angry with God. I cannot even remember everything I had said; but I know that I was infuriated and could not believe that He would allow me to go thru this situation again. I asked, "What have I done wrong this time, Lord?" I felt that I was being punished for something. I just could not understand why I could not have a "normal" life.

As I was drying my eyes, I realized I was driving like a maniac, and the car behind me had quickly slowed down to allow distance between us, because of my recklessness. I had lost it, right there in my car. I could not take it anymore. Losing my phone sent me overboard. I did not have money to buy another phone and that was my main source of communication. I just could not believe that God would allow me to fall—what I thought was so low—in that time of my life. I felt as though I was supposed to be at a certain level of success; but I did not realize, at the time, I was reacting under the "worldly" system. I felt that because I was at a certain age, I should have more than what I had, and I should have been stable and financially secure. God's supernatural spirit hit me hard, as I calmed down.

The spirit of conviction, instantly, consumed me with such intensity. I pulled up to the room and sat in the car, once again in tears, this time in humility and shame. I was ashamed of myself for carrying on like I was crazy when I knew that the Heavenly Father's plan for my life was NEVER to hurt me and NEVER to leave me. I knew that His purpose for my life is ALWAYS greater than what I could see. He has shown me time and time again. He reminded me of that in the same place I had forgotten....in the car! I asked the Lord to forgive me. But, you know what? He had already forgiven me; because He knew I was operating in the flesh, and sometimes, we have to be diligently brought back into the supernatural realm of life. Reality says, "Look at your situation, Rayna; you are a failure." But the Supernatural Realm says, "Rayna, you can do all things through Christ who strengthens you!"

It is in the challenging moments that greater faith and joy, in the Lord is developed!!! The comfort of God's love calmed my spirit and caused me to fall into meditation of His sovereignty. In the midst of meditation, I began to worship Him which brought a spirit of praise over me. I praised Him for all the other times He had brought me out when I did not see the way thru. I praised Him for making a way for me to have money to pay for the room we had; because I did not know what I was going to do without any finances flowing in. I praised Him for my children sticking, closely, by my side when I needed them the most. I praised Him for protecting us and blessing us to, at least, be in a very nice and clean hotel room. I praised Him for His amazing grace and mercy. My attitude had shifted from "Lord, why me" to "Lord, thank you for choosing me." He is a great God and I am so thankful to be in His presence, thru it ALL.

He comforted me and gave me His strength to get out of the car and go back into the room in FAITH that this WILL NOT be my life's circumstances forever, in this land. His Word says, "Thy kingdom come; thy will be done in earth as it is in heaven." My spirit interprets that as what He has ordained for me in heaven, which is royalty, is what He desires for me to have here IN *earth*— *IN* this temple called my life. He has so much more for me and for you, as well.

The Father knows you will get frustrated, angry and cry, at times; but He promised you that He will never leave or forsake you. He comforts you thru the most challenging times, in your life, just as you comfort your loved ones when they are in their challenges. Just think of how much you love your babies or your mother and father; you will go to the ends of the earth for them. There is nothing that you would not do for them, according to God's will. Now just think about how much more the Heavenly

Father loves and desires to do for you. Life is not always going to be a piece of cake, but just know that you can find comfort in our Father God. He never stops loving you, even when it feels like He has left your side. He is still there watching over you. He is the God of comfort and whatever else you need Him to be, for you, thru this journey called life.

After calming down and taking the groceries in, I went to my car to look for my phone, again. My attitude about the situation took a total turn for the good. I said, "Lord, please have mercy." As soon as I finished the last word, my text message alert sounded! My phone was plastered to the side of the car panel between the seats. I know I had looked there (or at least I thought I did) when I was searching for it the first time, but it was not there. I began to praise God for His grace. He comforts me even thru the times I cry and throw fits! His grace and love comforted my spirit.

The bottom line is that God will ALWAYS be there for you when no one else could; because He lives IN you! His name is made great thru you. His glory is revealed in the most trying seasons of your life. Even when it hurts the most, allow Him to use you for His glory. Remember, someone is watching to see how you will react when your back is pressed against the wall, especially when you have ministered to them about trusting the Lord. At times, you will cry and break down; but pick yourself back up, quickly, and keep it pushing. God makes no mistakes and He knows what is best for you even when it seems as if it is the worst. Trust Him and walk in His direction. He will lead you into your destiny, in Jesus name. Amen. Joshua 1:9; Matthew 6:9-10

MY SOUL PROVIDER

I have not always been saved
and living the example of Christ
I have not always been kind
and extremely nice

I have not always been honest
and filled with truth
I have not always allowed
Him to lead me thru

I have not always been
meek, humble and caring
I have not always been giving
and open to sharing

I have not always been coherent
and wise to His Word
I have not always listened
when I said I have heard

I have not always walked in
truth and lived a righteous life
I have not always had this
spirit that shines by His light

Yet, I have always had a
love so pure and true
Who is always there no
matter what I go thru

I have always had a trustworthy
faithful and genuine friend
Who has always been there
from the very beginning

I was always offered His
sovereign spirit of peace
Who allows my mind and
soul to rest in tranquility

I have always had a
covering thru the night and day
He who covers me by His
precious mercy and grace

I have always had Him
as my burden bearer
He has always been my
heavy load carrier

I have always had Jesus but
my sins had blinded me
He shed his blood for you and me
when He died at Calvary

I have always had
the Holy son of man
Who has strategically
designed my destiny's plan

January 28, 2012
Matthew 16:25

Chapter 12

Standing On His Promises

What the Lord says He will do...it WILL be done. Our Father is not a liar. At times we cannot see, with our physical eyes, how it is going to happen; but when we are walking in the presence of our Heavenly Father, we begin to see with our spiritual eyes—Faith. Faith believes against everything that is contrary to the Word of God. If He says you are more than a conqueror then that is just who you are. It does not matter how bad the situation may seem or the doubt that negative people try so hard to drown you with... You are more than a conqueror! The Lord knows your needs and desires and His word says that He will supply ALL of them when we seek Him first. He does not retract on His Word.

It was the end of August 2017, and my youngest son was in the Marine boot camp, when I was preparing for his graduation. Everything seemed to be going well until five days before his big day. My older son's car had broken down. His car was the only source of transportation we had, at the time. My car had been repossessed about three weeks after we moved into the hotel; which the Lord had blessed me to keep it until we found a place to stay. Anyway, my son told me that we were going to have to "chance it" with his car so we could make it to his brother's graduation. I told him that I did not think driving his car would be a good idea. He then aggressively asked me, "Well, how are we going to get there, momma?" I responded, "I don't know, but we WILL get there." He stared at me, rolled his eyes and walked off. I knew my Father was not going to let me down! He knew we desired to be there to show support and to congratulate my son for his awesome accomplishments. I just knew He would not let me down! The days seemed like they were passing by very quickly. My son's (the graduate) girlfriend called me to see if the logistics had been worked out; and I told her no. I am sure she became nervous even though she said she was not because she texted me again later that evening. I told her the same thing I had told my son…. we WILL get there; even though I did not know how, at that moment. I just knew without a doubt that we were going to be there.

It came down to the day it was time to leave and I still had no clue how we were going to visit my son. So I got up early that morning and when everyone left, I sat in the bed and I began to praise God with all my might. And as I was praising him I heard, "Call your Uncle Freddie." I opened my eyes and sat there for a minute. I knew it was the Holy Spirit that had spoken to me, because I would have never even thought to call my uncle. I was so nervous, but I had to be obedient. So, I called my Uncle Freddie and told him my situation; and I asked him if he knew of any military assistance I could request seeing how he had been in the air force for many years. He told me he would call me back after he finished his errands. When he called back, he said he would help me with a portion of the cost. It was exactly what I needed! I had just enough money to rent a car so we could be there for my son! Thank you, again, for your kindness and generosity, Uncle Freddie. I will never forget how you blessed me and my family. It was and still is truly appreciated! We got the rental car two hours before it was time to get on the road to travel to South Carolina……TWO HOURS!!! The Lord even blessed us to get an upgrade and to keep the car an extra day!!!

God is a RIGHT IN TIME God!! He never goes back on His promises…. NEVER! I know that I can always depend on Him to do what He says He WILL do. It is up to me to have *faith* in knowing that He will do it. Faith is so powerful; it moves the Lord! Yes, I was in a hotel room at that very moment, writing this book! And as I was writing, my strength was growing; because I knew God's purpose for my life was much greater than the situation I was in. Hallelujah! I know that my life is not my own and that experience is a testimony to someone who is lacking faith in the Master. It is also a testimony to someone who is about to go thru or is going thru, at this very moment, the same experience. I am here to tell you *do not give up on our Heavenly Father*! Stand on His promises for your life. You will overcome!

God will not leave you alone or forsake you. Even when nervousness and fear come upon you, PRAISE right on thru it. The enemy does not want you to prosper; and he does not want you to walk in your God given rights and abilities. I came to tell you to shake the enemy off with your praise and worship. When you get frustrated and angry, PRAISE THE LORD! When you are confused and scared, PRAISE THE LORD! PRAISE HIM when you are stressed and worn out from the cares of this world. PRAISE HIM, ANYHOW, in Jesus name. His strength will bring you thru. You cannot make it on your own strength, because it is of the flesh. You need a supernatural strength....GOD'S STRENGTH! He will not only give you His strength thru the most challenging storms of your life; but He will endow you with His joy, compassion, comfort and, most of all, His everlasting love. Never give up, on the Father, no matter how bad it seems. He has not left you to stand on your own. Keep your hand in His hand so you may see His greatness in your life. He is "THE GOD OF HIS WORD", in Jesus mighty and holy name. Amen. Isaiah 41:10

*You were a Spirit being before you
were a Human being. And if you dwell
in the nature of the Most High God, then
you will come to realize that you are more
powerful, thru His spirit, than what the world
has led you to believe.*

REFLECTIONS

I'm standing here starring into the
mirror of my soul and what do I see
I see the spirit of the most high
God starring right back at me

I see His spirit of *Wisdom* which
teaches me the righteousness I know
I see the spirit of *Discernment* which
directs me in the path I should go

I see *Grace* which is His unmerited favor
given to me not because it is deserved
I see *Mercy* which is His divine
protection that keeps me covered

I see the spirit of *Sovereignty*
that is greater than any other god
I see the spirit of *Faith* which has
the ability to believe against all odds

I see the spirit of *Authority* which
allows me to speak life into a dead situation
I see *Dominion* that the Father purposely
gave to me at the beginning of creation

I see the spirit of *Perseverance* which allows
me to press forward thru the treacherous storms
I see *Endurance* which is His divine strength
given to accept the trials that are out of the norm

I see the spirit of *Kindness* which is
sweet compassion He gives towards others
I see *Forgiveness* which softens the heart to
let go of grudges against my sisters and brothers

I see the spirit of *Peace* that is a gentle
silence that surpasses all understanding
I see *Humbleness* which is a heart of
humility that is always gradually expanding

I see the spirit of *Holiness* which strives
to live in the righteousness of Christ
I see *Gratefulness* which is a
joyful heart; thanking God for my life

I see the spirit of *Power* which is
total control that He holds in His hands
And I see the spirit of unconditional *Love*
which is what He has for me that I may live again

March 2014
Galatians 5:25

Chapter 13

Winner

It was a Sunday afternoon when my family and I were at Dave and Busters for my grandson's birthday party. My god son kept insisting that I compete with him on the basketball game; and of course, I accepted the challenge! Let's just say I won the majority of the games; and he could not stand it! When the next day had come, my god son continued to talk about me winning the game. He could not stand the fact that I won more games than he did! I knew it was a "guy" thing! So he went on to say, "Ok Auntie, we need to find a basketball court." Now if you knew me, you would know that I am not a quitter, nor am I intimidated by a righteous challenge; especially from a child who is still growing into himself. There is *always* a lesson that could be learned in a situation like this!

Being who I am, I accepted his challenge. I also informed him that although I may not be able to play the game like him, I will definitely give him a run for his money with my shooting skills! Then he boosted himself and said in a sarcastic voice, "Alright Auntie, alright", as if I was supposed to have gotten scared because he said that! I said to him, "I have confidence in myself." My middle son, who was listening, interrupted the conversation and sarcastically said, "What does confidence have to do with it?" "It's basketball…." My god son fell on the floor laughing like that was so funny. I began to make a comment to my son, but then the Holy Spirit came over me and stopped me. I thought, "This particular instance showed that both of them were immature." My son missed the entire lesson that I was trying to teach to my god son and to him.

You see, the whole point was that winning is not always being in first place, even though the world has some of us convinced that it is. Winning is having the confidence (FAITH) to make the move no matter who or what you are up against. I am sure my fourteen-year old athletic god son could beat me in a game of basketball. I have not been on a court in years! But the reason why I accepted his challenge was for him to understand that my determination and effort had already made me a winner whether I won 1st Place or 5th Place…. the fact of the matter is I would have won a Place. I could have allowed him to intimidate me and not accept the challenge at all; but first, I am too stubborn for that; and second, God did not give me a spirit of fear! I could have just backed out of the challenge, but if I did, I would not have had a chance to place at all. I use instances like this to teach valuable lessons to my children; and I pray that they receive what is being taught.

That was not the first time my god son had challenged me— Uno, typing contest, cooking (now he should have known better than that!), and now this basketball stuff! What my god son still has not realized is that every time he tries to challenge me with his ego and pride, he loses. But, when he humbles himself and realizes that he is playing against someone who is seasoned in a myriad of areas, he tends to get off of his high-horse and pay more attention to mastering the game instead of beating the person. Oh, but there is a difference!

You see when you are just out to *beat* someone, more than likely, your focus stays on the person and what they are doing. You are watching their lane and copying their strategy, instead of developing a strategy of your own; and now, you are all over the place, because you have no initial plan, for yourself, to win the game. But, when you choose to *master* the game, your vision becomes tunnel. Your focus changes from the opponent to the strategy…. your strategy. Your diligence is ignited and all you can visualize is the *game.* Now, ego and pride, which kept you distracted, has left the building and confidence (FAITH) has entered!

This is the part my son missed. FAITH (confidence) is *always* essential in everything that we do. He studies and indulges in stocks and options. If he did not believe that he could master the art of trading, then, he would not have even bothered to learn the strategy. If you do not believe you can achieve something, then that is what will become real in your mind, and finally manifest in your life.

If there is anything that I desire to do, I speak it and believe it, no matter what anyone think or say about me. No one can discourage me from my goals nor dreams but me, and God's grace will not allow me to do so; because I have found who I am in the Lord.

When you discover who the Heavenly Father really is to you, then, will you discover who you are in Him! You are Victory because He is the VICTOR! Oh yes, He is, in Jesus name! Amen.
Romans 8:37

*Every season is planting season.
You must trust the Lord God
to lead you to fertile ground!*

THRU IT ALL TRUST GOD

Thru your trials and tribulations
you say, "how do I keep going
when it feels as though I am not
reaping the good I have been sowing

How do I continue to love when
love has been taken away from me
How do I walk this tedious journey when
these carnal eyes keep distracting me

How do I lay my head to slumber
when at night I cannot rest
How do I continue to give my all when
I feel as though I have given my best

How do I pick up the broken part of me
when it has been shattered to pieces
How do I continue to be obedient to the
Word and the righteousness it teaches

Jesus said he has overcome the world
therefore, He wants you to be of good cheer
He wants you to trust Him thru your trying
times and trust Him thru your fears

Trust Him when your highs are
low and when your ups are down
Trust Him when you are doubtful
and when loneliness abounds

Trust Him thru your pain and tears
and thru your sorrow and grief
Trust Him thru your misunderstandings
your heartaches and your disbelief

Trust Him on your good and bad days
your better and worse days too
Trust He is God and God all by Himself
and He knows the plans He has just for you

July 30, 2011
Jeremiah 29:11

Chapter 14

Moving Into The New Me

It was Thursday November 9, 2017 at 12:46am and I was sitting at the table, in the hotel, writing the final chapter of this book. I had been praying and seeking the Lord about how to end it; because, I guess, I was hoping to say that I had moved into my home. I guess I was hoping for this big spectacular ending for the book; but I had come to accept sometimes that was not the way God had ordained it for the moment. But, just because I had not moved into my home, yet, did not mean that I was not going to move at all!

You see, I used the word *moving* in the title because the word *move* means to change the place or position of; but when the *ing* is added, it means in *motion*. I had been preparing to move because I knew the Heavenly Father had my best interest at heart. I knew He had the right place waiting just for me. I had not even unpacked my bags, because I KNEW that was not my final stop. He allowed the eviction process to happen because it was time for me to press forward and excel in my God-given purpose. Sometimes, the Lord allows the challenges to come, in order to rekindle the fire in us, to remind us of our purpose. I had become too comfortable and was procrastinating on what He had instructed me to do. I only had two months left on the lease; and at the time, I could not understand why He would allow an eviction. But thru it all, I faithfully trusted and still trust Him to the very end. And not only was I sitting there writing the last chapter of the book He instructed me to write months ago, but He has blessed me to use the very trial I was going thru to be my testimony of Faith!

When I was evicted from my apartment, I only took our clothes and a few boxes with me. My son had a small storage that he, graciously, allowed me to store the extra boxes I had. All of my furniture was left behind, because I had no place to store it. The picture on the book cover is actually some of my furniture and belongings that were placed in the parking lot of the complex the day the Sheriff's department came to execute the writ. On that day, I cried, uncontrollably, when we came here to the hotel. The only thing that was going thru my mind was how hard I had worked to pay for my apartment and my belongings; and now, I was stuck in that freaking hotel, again. The Lord allowed me to throw my pity party; but it was not long, at all, before He had shut it down and reminded me of the vision of His promises and purpose for my life. I had to move from there because He orchestrated it that way. It was not in my timing—when I thought I should move—yet in HIS perfect timing…. when He knew it was best for me to move.

When you are planning to move to a new place, you tend to give away or throw away a lot of the old things you have because you know that you are going to want new items for your new home. Some things you try to hold on to because you have had it for so long, when really, you know that it is time to let go of it. And if you are downsizing, you definitely have to get rid of more than what you probably bargained for because there would not be room to store it where you are going. It will only *clutter* the new space you are moving into.

When God is excelling you into another level of His realm, it is the same as moving into a new place. You have to rid some things, habits, thoughts and even people out of your life. And as you remove people, forgive them, because forgiveness is essential in moving forward with the Lord. God NEVER moves you into the exact same thing. It may look similar but there is always something or someone new He has there, awaiting you. There is always a new learning experience in every situation or place He takes you to, ALWAYS! Your life is not your own. If you do not believe me, you can read anywhere in the new testament, of the bible, about Jesus starting from when he was born (Luke 2:8-11). He came to set the example, for us, of how to live by faith. Everything He had done, every blessing and every miraculous work He had performed was solely on FAITH in our Father. You do know that we have the same Father, right?! But the ultimate reason our Heavenly Father sent the son of man was for Him to give His life that we may have life, and it more abundantly.

God uses us, as vessels, to do His mighty works. He moves thru us if we allow Him to dwell in us. He desires to do great things, thru us, because that is how He shows Himself to be the great and mighty GOD, in Jesus Name! Amen. Ephesians 4:20-24

And then it happened..........

He reigns on the mountain top and in the lowest valley. No matter where you are in life; you are still at his feet!

SOUND DIRECTION

In the past, I have turned
several corners that led me astray
To the point that you would not have
wanted to know me back in the day.

I was searching for direction
in all the wrong places
It seemed as though I was going in circles
because I kept seeing the same "old" faces.

I saw the face of doubt
who kept me walking in fear
I saw the face of negativity
who kept whispering in my ear.

I saw the face of poverty who
told me I would always be nothing
I saw the face of depression who made
me feel like my life was totally crumbling.

I saw the face of manipulation
who played tricks with my mind
I saw the face of deception who made me
feel that doing the right thing was a crime.

I saw the face of anger who
made me mad within my soul
I saw the face of defeat who would
never allow me to reach my goals.

I saw the face of complacency who did
not want me to venture off of its street
Because it knew if I walked a little
farther, new faces I would meet.

So I kept walking to end of the
block and I saw a face that was vague
It knew I could not see clearly, in the distance
so it waved and said, "Hello, my name is FAITH."

As I got closer, I saw its face had a divine
smile and it walked with a gentle stride
It said, "Today, I'll take you on a new road
and don't worry, I'll be your tour guide."

As I was walking with Faith, I met a new face called
Grace—who gives me favor beyond any measure
And as I continued on the road, I looked up
and told Grace thank you for the gesture.

I met the face of Wisdom
who teaches me what I know
I met the face of Discernment who
guides my decisions in a righteous flow.

I met the face of Forgiveness
who lets go of all the past
I met the face of Patience who tells me
to slow down when I am moving too fast.

I met the face of Peace who
keeps my spirit settled and calm
I met the face of Praise who, to the
Father, expresses its glorious psalms.

I met the face of Strength who
picks me up when I am weak
I met the face of Humbleness who
keeps my spirit quiet and meek.

And as my friend, Faith, continues to
lead me along with Mercy and Grace
I can be sure that I am walking in
sound direction with all the right faces!

December 20, 2017
2Timothy 1:7

It rains a lot just before the season changes. Rain nourishes the harvest for growth. Praise God for the rain!

Chapter 15

....By Faith

The Lord is truly a faithful and loving God! Never give up on the Lord because He will NEVER give up on you! As I said in chapter fourteen, just because I had not moved when I wrote it, did not mean that I was not going to move at all! Before I could even start to proofread the book, the Lord moved in my favor! When I found peace, in my spirit, to write what I thought was the last chapter; the Lord kept showing me one particular apartment complex. Moving in faith and obedience, I acted on the opportunity. My, oh my, I am so grateful that I did! The Lord gave me what I trusted Him for; to conclude this book of testimonies with a testimony of His spectacular blessings and amazing grace!

It was November 28th and my oldest son was getting on the plane to Chicago, IL for Navy boot camp training. I was headed into a job interview, when he called me to say farewell. After four hours of completing paperwork for the job only to realize I could not take it because of the time and lack of transportation, I missed my appointment to complete the application for an apartment. I did not have a vehicle, at the time, and my daughter had blessed me to use her car on that particular day. I was a little discouraged because I had missed the appointment. I was trying to save the money I had—which was not enough—to get the place. So, I did what I knew to do....I stepped out on FAITH and I called an Uber! I completed the paperwork and the same day I was told that there was a discrepancy; but within thirty minutes, the Lord had worked it all out for me! I did not even have all the money I needed to move in the apartment. I said, "Lord, you did not bring me this far to leave me now. You did not put this apartment in my spirit only not to give it to me." His Favor is priceless! My friend and all my children came together and blessed me to be able to move in my place three days after the application was approved!! Hallelujah! Thank you Jesus! And I was, actually, sitting on my brand new bed that my son purchased for me, writing the *real* final chapter of the book! The Lord knew my heart's desire and He honored it for me! He is such a loving God. He heard my request and He answered.....just like that! Even as I was writing chapter fourteen, I had Faith in my heart and my new home on my mind!

It is not about the home; yet, it is about *His Power* that is in the blessing! God desires to do so much more for us. He allows trials and challenges in our lives to not only draw closer *to* Him, but to draw *into* Him. He desires an intimate relationship with His children. He desires for us to be *in* tune with His Holy Spirit just as a fetus is attached to its mother, by the umbilical cord. The baby feels everything that the mother feels. It eats what the mother eats. It feels the very beat of her heart. That is how the Lord desires us to have intimacy with Him. We are not just the apple of His eye....we are much more than that to Him! He has done a brand new thing, in this land, and He wants to relocate us to a higher realm in His Glory. God desires for us to dwell in the realm of His heart because we are the very *beat* of His heart! Our God models parenting after His own loving ways. As parents to our babies, we desire to give them the best of everything, and so does the Lord who desires to give to His children, in abundance, and so much more!

An Intimate relationship with the Heavenly Father, which is first and foremost, along with faith and obedience bring about favor and an abundance of blessings. No matter what your circumstances are, have FAITH. No matter how devastating the situation may seem, have FAITH. No matter who have walked out of your life or who has given up on you, have FAITH. No matter how bad people talk about you or laugh at you, behind your back, have FAITH. Faith and obedience, in our Heavenly Father, is what has brought me thru all the years of challenges and trials. When I had nothing else to depend on and no one else to call on, I had my FAITH in my Father. And as I sat there on that today and reflected on all the times I thought it was over, He reminded me that HIS grace, by my FAITH in Him, brought me thru it all; and it will do the same for you, in Jesus name, Amen. Matthew 6:9-13

My prayer for you:

Father God, it is in the name of Jesus, that I speak FAITH into the spirit of Your people. Not only do I speak Faith, Father, but I also speak a renewing of their mind to receive Your Holy Spirit; and Your grace that will empower them to walk in obedience, by Faith. I speak Extraordinary Favor over their lives; and that You cover them and their families under your protection daily, in the name of Jesus. Father God, I speak your strength over them when they are weak and feel they cannot go any farther. Forgive them of their shortcomings and keep Your loving hands upon them. Be a shield all around them and keep them from the schemes and deceptions of the enemy. Mature their mind, their heart and their spirit. Grace them with Your compassion, Your sovereignty and Your mercy, Father God. Supply their every need; and fill them with Your truth so they may be saved and drawn into You, by Your grace, thru their Faith. Empower them with Your everlasting love so they may be able to witness to someone that is lost or confused. Use Your children, Father, to draw others into You. Touch, heal and deliver, Lord God. On behalf of Your people, I give You all the glory and all the honor, in Jesus Holy and Matchless name, Amen.

IN CHRIST JESUS,

You are Blessed, You are Highly Favored, You are Saved, You are Delivered, You have Joy, You have Peace, You have Love, You have Dominion, You are Strong, You are Healed, You are Healthy, You are Wise, You are Smart, You are Beautiful, You are Handsome, You are Restored, You are Wealthy, You are Prosperous, You are a Great Steward, You are More Than a Conqueror, You are a King, You are a Queen, You are the Very Beat of His Heart! YOU ARE VICTORY, in CHRIST JESUS! ***AMEN!***

CRAZY FAITH

They called me *Crazy* when I spoke
to things they could not physically see
So they labeled me as a nut case
and chose not to deal with me
Crazy! They said I am. Well
then, to them, crazy I will be!

They got mad when they could not
distract me with negativity and ignorance
They were furious when I kept moving and
when they could not break my resistance
And as I pressed forward, I still saw
their eyes on me from a distance

Yeah, they were criticizing me, ridiculing
my name, laughing around and joking
Yet I was still on my journey, getting closer to
receiving what I had believed and what He had spoken
While they were still in the same position
when I started this path….confused and broken

And because they could not see what I saw,
they insisted that I was walking into a tragedy
But I refused to listen to doubters
and I refused to let anyone stop me
Crazy! They said I am. Well
then, to them, crazy I will be!

Got to end of the road and the door
was wide open waiting just for me
They could not believe their eyes
as they ran towards me vigorously

But God shut the door just before they entered
and said, "You'll have to walk your own journey
Because remember, Crazy! You said she was!
And Crazy her FAITH shall forever be!"

December 20, 2017
Matthew 8:26-27

*"It is when we decide to rid ourselves of
worldly characteristics that the Heavenly
Father takes pleasure in filling us
up with His Kingdom Qualities."*

No one can put a value on you that is greater than the ONE who created you and has already paid the cost. And no one can devalue you either!

Special Dedication

I am dedicating this book to my beloved father who taught me so much about life and survival. He raised me with qualities that he only knew....masculine qualities! I use to think that he was so harsh on me, but as I have grown and matured, I have come to realize that it was beneficial for my life; because I was blessed to raise three biological sons of my own. I watched how dedicated and determined my father was to start his own business, and how he did not let anyone discourage him from his plans or dreams. His endurance and FAITH caused him to excel and prosper beyond measures. Pops, I miss you so much and I am extremely blessed to have called you my father. I know you are resting in love, daddy.

My good friend, Rev. Garland Brooks, wrote a poem to his beautiful daughter and it touched my heart because the inspiration he wrote to her is what my father ministered to me thru his life's journey. So without further a due, I present to you "Poem from Daddy to Kayla".

Don't think because I'm old, I can't relate
I am your Father, so don't hesitate.
Share all that is on your heart and mind
We both know that true love isn't blind.
Each day is a stepping stone to fulfill dreams
Finding out purpose and what life really means.
Setting goals, treading through with hope and fears
With smiles, joy, triumphs and even shedding of tears.
Always moving forward, never looking back
Determination and strength we'll never lack.
Throughout life, many questions will be asked
Stay laser-beamed focused on your given task.
Your dreams and goals you will always achieve
Just hold on, press in, trust God and BELIEVE!
The path we take is all about making a choice
Fight or run, love or hate and to be sad or rejoice!
It's all about you…Who you are in Jesus Christ
He's the author and finisher, the giver of life.
So choose to live, to love and to be free
Do not let society and the world have a hold on thee…
Because what we do from this day forth…..
Affects our Eternity!!!

Peace and Love, Daddy
08/15/2006

Book Review

"Moving Into The New Me...By Faith" is a book that I didn't realize I needed. I'm moving into a new me—transitioning from a young lady into a grown woman. This transition is one that no one speaks about so I didn't know it was a pivotal point in my life. It is confusing, challenging and easy, all at once. This book helped me to understand my transition; and ease into it fearlessly.

For example, the author said, "....He gracefully present opportunities so we may repent, reconcile, and redeem ourselves with Him..." This phrase helped me to understand so many things. There was this guy...it's always a guy right? LOL! I had a feeling he wasn't for me so I cut him off; but he kept coming back into my life. Before reading this phrase, I thought maybe God wanted me to be with him...LOL; but that was the "young lady" talking. The grown woman, in me, realized God was giving me an opportunity to redeem myself, with Him, by leaving that man alone. It's all becoming clearer now!

Another part of my journey is understanding the power I have within me. I know I have the power, but sometimes the conditioning from the world causes me to forget. Reading this book helps me to remember that there is not a request God cannot manifest. After all, He is the Creator of everything. When I read this, it made me think, wow, He really *is* the Creator of EVERYTHING! If He can create a sky, a sun, a moon, a SOLAR SYSTEM; why can't He bless me with my Benz? LOL! Seriously, it really made me quiet my mind and meditate upon the truth that our requests are so small compared to the greatness He has created! I'm sure He can't wait for us to be bold enough to request something enormous and beyond our thoughts.

When I read these stories of faith, it made me reminisce on my own stories. I like how it is so relatable. Reminiscing on those times are something I rarely do because I'm always looking toward the future. Taking a moment to think back has actually propelled me forward even more. All the little moments of mustard seeds of faith I've had has added up over time and has created a taller mustard plant! Thinking back of all the times God has had my back, when I wasn't paying attention, is really humbling. I am grateful for this book that brought forth the opportunity to reflect.

Chapter ten is my favorite! It is a bit similar to the present point of my journey. Focusing on the good and remaining one with God is what I'm practicing. It is not the easiest thing to do. Now that I think about it, it really is easy to do; however, there are just a lot of distractions as the author says, in the book. The situation, the people around you and the environment sometimes just does not add up to who I'm trying to become. Reading this chapter is a great reminder for me and it's comforting to know that I'm not the only one that is going through this phase. For me, it's a point of isolation. Remaining positive and focusing on God requires my isolation that nobody really understands. I feel like the author understands though.... she is my mom.

I had planned on writing a summary of every chapter of this book, but that would have given away the goods! Instead, I decided to do it this way. I'm not sure what point you are in, in your journey of life; maybe you have already reached your point of triumph or maybe you are just now entering the ring. No matter what phase of life you're in, "Moving Into The New Me...By Faith" will allow you to have a new perspective on your life and God. The poems are a great read when you only have a few minutes and need a quick reminder not to punch your coworker in face! And, the short stories are there for a great morning meditation.

I'm proud to say the author is my mommy; and I'm grateful to have read this book, at this point in my life. Really, no one told me about this part of womanhood. This transition is one that can be made or resisted. I've resisted this growth before but I'm not making that mistake again. I wasn't sure what was happening to me until my mommy told me "you're in your prime, you're becoming a woman." Reading this book has made me reflect on my life and realize that everything is only chapters adding up to an amazing read just as "Moving Into The New Me....By Faith".

So don't stress, remain focused on God, know that you have the power within you, and enjoy creating your own great story! This book will minister to all the right people and a few of the wrong ones too! I love you mommy and keep on changing lives!

-Chan Phillips

BIBLIOGRAPHY

Zondervan Quest NIV Study Bible, General Editors, Marshall Shelley (1994); Phyllis Ten Elshof (2003), Rev. Ed., Zondervan, 2003

The King James Version Bible: Containing the Old and New Testaments, Thomas Nelson Bibles, 2003

New International Version. Biblica, 2011.BibleGateway.com,www.biblegateway.com/versions/New-International-Version-NIV-Bible/

ORDER INFORMATION

First Book: God's Words Plain and Simple
A book of poetry that is healing medicine for the soul!

Order on author's website at:
www.authorraynastephens.com

Author's Contact Information:
Email: info@authorraynastephens.com

www.ingramcontent.com/pod-product-compliance
Lightning Source LLC
Chambersburg PA
CBHW071408290426
44108CB00014B/1735